DOG TRAINING GUIDE

MY DOG BECAME AN ANGEL

How To Speak So Your Dog Will Listen For All Dog Breeds

ANGEL MEADOWS

Copyright © 2021 Angel Meadows

All Rights Reserved

Copyright 2021 By Angel Meadows - All rights reserved.

The following book is produced below with the goal of providing information that is as accurate and reliable as possible. Regardless, purchasing this eBook can be seen as consent to the fact that both the publisher and the author of this book are in no way experts on the topics discussed within and that any recommendations or suggestions that are made herein are for entertainment purposes only. Professionals should be consulted as needed prior to undertaking any of the action endorsed herein.

This declaration is deemed fair and valid by both the American Bar Association and the Committee of Publishers Association and is legally binding throughout the United States.

Furthermore, the transmission, duplication or reproduction of any of the following work including specific information will be considered an illegal act irrespective of if it is done electronically or in print. This extends to creating a secondary or tertiary copy of the work or a recorded copy and is only allowed with express written consent from the Publisher. All additional right reserved.

The information in the following pages is broadly considered to be a truthful and accurate account of facts and as such any inattention, use or misuse of the information in question by the reader will render any resulting actions solely under their purview. There are no scenarios in which the publisher or the original author of this work can be in any fashion deemed liable for any hardship or damages that may befall them after undertaking information described herein.

Additionally, the information in the following pages is intended only for informational purposes and should thus be thought of as universal. As befitting its nature, it is presented without assurance regarding its prolonged validity or interim quality. Trademarks that are mentioned are done without written consent and can in no way be considered an endorsement from the trademark holder.

Table of Contents

Chapter 1: Leash Training 8

    Understanding the Urge to Explore 8

    The Proper Tools 9

    Stop Technique 11

Chapter 2: Simple Training 14

    Proofing Training 14

    Sit 19

    Down 22

Chapter 3: Intermediate Training 26

    Take It/Drop It 26

    Off 28

    Quiet 29

Chapter 4: Advanced Training 31

    Gentle 31

    Wait 33

    Leave It 35

Chapter 5: Puppy Training Basics 38

    After Bringing Your Puppy Home 59

    Introducing the New Dog 61

    Have Realistic Expectations 63

    Practice Makes Perfect 64

Chapter 6: House Training and Problem Behaviors 67

- Biting 67
- Whining and Crying 71
- House Training 74

Chapter 7: Socialization Training 79
- Socialization Benefits 79
- Early Socialization 80
- Positivity is Key 83
- Socialization Tips and Tricks 84

Chapter 8: Crate Training 87
- Crating Basics 88
- Getting Started 89
- Introducing Isolation 90
- Crate Tips 93

Conclusion 95

Chapter 1: Leash Training

Understanding the Urge to Explore

The truth is that your puppy isn't trying to dominate you, but something much more genuine and simple: dogs love the outdoors and exploring. The outside world is a wonder for dogs, and walks provide them with both physical and mental stimulation because of this. There are so many sights and sounds for them to explore, and sometimes they get ahead of themselves, or rather they get ahead of you. They aren't pulling you out of any malicious intent; they are simply enjoying themselves so much that they can think of little else but continuing to explore. This is an incredibly strong desire for your puppy, so even when a dog is well-trained, they still might struggle. Thankfully, with leash training, you can help your puppy learn to overcome these overwhelmingly strong desires. With much practice, they can learn to walk beside you without pulling you along the way.

It is important to mention that at times your puppy might struggle more with this than at other times. You may think your puppy is full leash trained, and then at some point, they may start pulling again seemingly out of the blue. This is not a failure of training, but simply a natural part of growth and maturity. Simply go back to practicing some leash training, and before long, your puppy should be reminded how to walk on the leash properly.

The Proper Tools

Even if you don't believe your puppy is going to grow big enough to pull you on a leash, having proper leash training is a vital aspect of safety. By teaching your puppy to walk on a leash correctly, not only will they not injure you, but they won't injure themselves, either. This is always really important, but you will find it especially vital in intense situations. Whether there is an emergency at home or your dog simply sees another animal coming near, by having your puppy properly leash trained, you can keep them under control in a potentially difficult situation.

If your puppy is a large breed, you might be tempted to get a prong collar when they get older, but I urge you not to do this. Prong collars are inhumane and extremely dangerous. Thankfully, there are some much better options that can help with leash pulling, even by larger breeds.

A good all-purpose tool, no matter the size of your dog, is a chest-led harness unlike other harnesses, which attaches the leash onto the back between the shoulder blades, the chest-led harness hooks in the front. This is great, a back-led harness it is able to reduce pulling. When your dog attempts to pull, due to the angle of the leash attachment, it will cause your puppy to turn around, rather than allowing them to freely pull forward. This is also a safer method than using a collar for your dog, as they won't be able to choke or strangle themselves if they get worked up and start pulling or chasing after something. Simply put, the chest-led harness prioritizes safety for both human and canine.

If your puppy grows into an especially big and strong dog, then a chest-led harness might not be enough. Ideally, you will have full leash trained your puppy by this point, but that isn't always possible. In that case, you may want to consider a head collar. This type of collar works in much the way a halter does on a horse. If your dog attempts to pull on it, then instead of being allowed to pull forward, the dog will simply bring their head around, stopping their progress. These are not only great for especially large breeds, but also for the elderly, disabled, or pregnant to avoid strenuous pulling. Keep in mind your puppy will have to be habituated to a harness, leash, and collar with plenty of praise, rewards, time, and patience. This is especially true if you use a head collar.

Stop Technique

When training your puppy to not pull, one simple and great method is the stop technique. This method is incredibly easy to use and understand, but also effective in many cases, as your puppy will quickly see that pulling gets them nowhere. Quite literally. To practice, the stop technique walk with your puppy down a sidewalk. If your puppy starts to pull forward, don't reinforce it by following after them. Instead, stop dead in your tracks. This will make your puppy see that the consequence of pulling is that they don't get to go where they want, that they are forced to wait and be patient. Don't wait for your puppy to be pulling hard against the leash to practice this technique. Instead, the moment they start to pull on the leash stop in your tracks. Once the leash goes slack from your puppy sitting down or taking a step back, you can praise them and continue on your way. Repeat this every single time your puppy pulls on the leash so that they learn that pulling never gets them what they want.

If simply stopping doesn't work, then try taking them even further away from their goal when they pull. To do this, every time your puppy pulls on the leash, use the command phrase 'let's go,' turn in the opposite direction, and walk.

When doing this, you want to use an excited voice to get your puppy's focus on you, so that they will come along. You shouldn't pull or yank them along, but rather have them follow you. When they are following you with the leash relaxed, then you can go back to your original direction.

You may have to repeat this process a few times before they give up on pulling, but before long, your puppy will understand what you are communicating—that pulling won't be rewarded.

Remember to encourage your puppy to walk beside you without pulling; you should give them plenty of rewards and treats. In the early stages, this means you should give them regular rewards as they are walking without pulling. You can then slowly phase out the rewards, but still, remember to give them praise when they do well. Whenever your puppy goes through a normal stubbornness streak during their growth process, use frequent rewards and the anti-pulling techniques here to remind them of their training.

Chapter 2: Simple Training

Proofing Training

Before you get to work on training your dog new commands, it is important that you understand the process of proofing. This method is a part of the training process, which should be used every time you teach your dog something new. While we are starting this chapter by discussing proofing, it is actually the last step in training a command.

When you train your dog to learn a new command, many people will practice in the same areas and circumstances. For instance, if your routine is to practice in the living room, you will likely continue to practice there. But, while your dog may comply with your commands in this scenario, many people soon learn that is not enough. The problem with this is that your dog only learns to practice the command in that specific environment, so you must teach them to comply in other situations, as well. A good example of this is telling your dog to 'come.' For many people, they will train their dog to use this command, but then their dog will only use it when there aren't any other distractions. If they ask the dog to come to the dog park or when the dog wants something, then there is little to no chance of the dog complying. But, with proofing, you train your dog in a variety of circumstances, so that even when there are more distractions, your dog will learn to ignore them and do as you ask.

To understand how this works, you must think like a dog. If you teach your dog to 'come' when you are in your own home, then they will be able to comply at home. But, if you try to tell your dog to 'come' at the park, they will be confused and likely won't understand what you want. This is because while you may be saying 'come,' what the dog understands is you saying 'come to me when we're at home.' Because of this, your dog won't understand, even if you are using the same command as usual. This is why proofing is important. By practicing a command in a variety of places and circumstances, you can teach your dog that 'come' is not impacted by outside variables. That 'come' always means 'come to me' and not 'come to me when certain circumstances align.'

Whenever you begin training your dog a new command, you want to do so in a quiet and controlled indoor environment without distractions. While it may be nice to practice training outside when the weather is nice, this should only be done when proofing and not when teaching the new commands.

The reason for this is because there are many more distractions outside, from sights, sounds, and smells to squirrels and birds your dog may want to chase. When you practice inside, you can ensure that the environment has fewer stimulants for your dog's senses, so that they can focus fully on your training.

Once your dog masters a given command or task in a controlled environment without distractions, it is then time to throw in a few of those distractions you were previously avoiding.

For this step, you should start slowly and be patient. Your dog will make more mistakes, but that is to be expected and nothing to be frustrated over. If your dog doesn't comply with a specific distraction added in, then try easing up slightly on the distractions and going at a slower pace.

There are many different distractions you can use. Try having another person or animal come into the room, add in some loud noises, have children run around and play, drop stuff onto the floor, or walk around the room rather than standing in place. Consider things your dog is easily distracted by, and try adding those into the proofing exercise. In time, your dog should learn to continue complying with your commands, no matter what distractions you throw in.

Again, take this slowly. It takes a lot of mental practice and works for a dog to build-up to this. It is much harder than most people imagine. It would be much like putting a chocolate cake in a child's room and telling them not to eat it. Most children would give in and eat the cake. But, if this was regularly practiced and the child learned they would be more greatly rewarded if they refrained, then they could learn in time. This means that if you want your dog to properly resist the distractions, you throw at them, you must appropriately reward them when they succeed. Resisting temptation must be worth it in the end, and the way you make it rewarding is by giving them their favorite treats or toys.

After your dog masters practicing the command with distractions, then it is time to practice in new environments. As we previously said, a dog can be confused, thinking that commands are only meant to be followed in a specific location. To show your dog that this is not true, you need to practice training in as many locations as possible. In the backyard, front yard, on a balcony, at a friend's house, in the park.

Remember that if you are in an area that isn't fenced in, then you should always keep your dog on a long leash. You can do this, even if you want to practice the stay or come commands, as there are leashes more than long enough. If you shop online, you can get leashes up to fifty feet long. By using a long leash, you can give your dog the freedom to freely practice any command while still ensuring everyone is kept safe.

Remember to be patient, keep training sessions to no more than ten minutes, and stay positive and upbeat. If you begin to get frustrated, your dog will sense it, and it will affect their abilities.

Whenever you take your dog out of the house, try to find places where you can practice proofing your training. For instance, you may ask your dog to sit or heel while on a walk, to lay down or stay at the vet, quiet, or calm at the pet store. There are many ways you can practice proofing your training in everyday life. Once your dog learns to consistently comply with a command in any environment, then you can consider their training of that command proofed.

Keep in mind that one of the biggest problems when it comes to dog training is inconsistency. If you find your dog won't proof a command, sometimes they will comply, and sometimes they won't; it may be because you or another person in the dog's life is being inconsistent. For instance, if the dog is generally not allowed on the bed, but sometimes you give in, then it creates confusion in the dog. If you are patient when giving commands and wait for your dog to do as you say, but another person gives up and lets the dog get away with not complying, then the dog will learn that they only have to comply when they feel like it. If you want to train your dog, it is vital that you and anyone else in your dog's life are consistent.

Talk with everyone in your household and consider making a list of dog rules. This will help everyone stay on the same page so that you can all be consistent.

Sit

Sit is one of the most basic of commands, as it is often the first command many dogs learn. This is for a good reason; it is not just a command for a fun trick, but one with many practical uses. You can use this if you need your dog to sit at attention and stay put whether at home, at the vet, or anywhere else; you can have them sit if they are in your way; or you can have them sit to be still before you feed them, load them into the car, or attach a leash. But that is not all. In the previous chapter, we talked about redirecting a dog's focus onto you so that they will better listen to commands and sit a great way to redirect focus.

Because it is such an easy and all-purpose command, dogs tend to have a lot of practice with it, making it an easier command for them to act on even when they are distracted. Once you have them seated, you can then give them another command, if needed.

Teaching a dog the sit command is incredibly easy. Follow these few steps:

- Hold a treat in your hand directly above your dog's nose. Your dog will puzzle out how to get the treat from your hand. To do this, they may paw and lick at the treat, or even whine. But, don't give them the treat until they sit.

- The moment your dog sits down, give them the treat. Repeat this process a few times until they begin automatically sitting to get the treat.

- Now, start saying the word 'sit' as your dog completes the action, following it up with the treat. Repeat this a few times, so that they come to associate the word 'sit' with the action.

- Practice this regularly until your dog sits on command whenever you ask. Find different ways to can implement this command in everyday life so that your dog learns to act on it whenever you ask, no matter the circumstances. You might have them sit before feeding them, before taking them on a walk, or before you throw a toy for them.

If your dog develops a habit of sitting down and then standing right back up, and your vet doesn't believe it is caused by pain, then you can lengthen the time they sit. Often times, when dogs do this, it is because they think they'll get the treat if they sit, no matter how short the time is. To overcome this practice training the command like this:

- Tell your dog to sit. Once they do sit, don't praise them or reward them if they stand right back up.

- Instead, if they stand back up, hide the treat behind your back and say the words 'uh-oh.' This phrase should be used to let your dog know whenever they make a mistake.

- Wait a couple of seconds after saying 'uh-oh,' and then remove the treat from behind your back and tell them to sit again. Make your dog sit for at least a few seconds before you treat them. Practice this regularly so that your dog learns to sit for longer periods.

- Later, you might consider teaching your dog 'okay' or another release word, so that they know they are at ease and free to stop sitting whenever you give them the cue.

Cautions:

- Keep in mind that training sessions should always be short, no more than fifteen minutes. But, less time if your dog has a limited attention span.

- For many large dogs and dogs with health conditions, it can be uncomfortable to sit for long periods. Don't push your dog to sit for longer than is comfortable. If your dog struggles with this, you can transition them into a down position after they sit.

- Never force your dog into a sitting position, as this can be harmful and cause injury. Allow them to figure it out on their own; they're smart enough.

- If your dog snaps at or attempts to force the food out of your hand, then use a toy instead of food. This also works better with dogs that are more toy-motivated than food-motivated.

Down

Once your dog learns how to sit, you can move onto the 'down' command. This is another simple command, but it does take a little more patience than the 'sit' command. All the same, it is an incredibly helpful command, as you can have your dog where you need them, but it is easier on their joints than sitting for long periods. This is especially true for larger and elderly dogs, who are more prone to joint pain from sitting.

Another great purpose for this command is if you need your dog to settle down in their crate, on a bed, or in the car, you can give them the 'down' command.

To teach 'down,' follow these steps:

- Hold a treat in your hand and give the 'sit' command.

- Once your dog sits, place your hand with the treat in your palm on the floor, so that the treat is hidden between your hand and the floor. Allow your dog to sniff the treat, but don't let them take it.

- Just like when your dog was learning to 'sit,' they will paw at or lick your hand, trying to figure out what they must do to get the treat.

- While puzzling out what to do, your dog will likely lay down in order to get a better angle for the treat. The moment they are lying down, praise them, and give them the treat.

- Repeat this process several times until your dog is sitting reliably. Once they are, begin pairing the word 'down' with the action of them lying down. Again, repeat this multiple times so that your dog connects the word with the action.

- Now, begin adding in a hand signal. To do this, give the command word as they are lying down while simultaneously lowering the other hand without a treat palm-side down. Repeat this process of using the command and the hand signal multiple times, giving your dog a chance to tie together the action, word, and hand signal.

- Practice using the command word, and the hand signal before your dog ever starts to lay down. When they comply, reward them.

- Try adding in the release word of 'okay' when your dog is free to be at ease.

If this method doesn't work with your dog, try using a treat or something else motivating. Your dog might also not comply if they don't feel safe in an environment, so be sure to practice somewhere they don't perceive any dangers.

Cautions:

- Never force your dog into the down position.

- Never punish your dog for not understanding or getting it wrong. If your dog doesn't comply, say 'uh-oh,' wait a couple of seconds, and try again.

Chapter 3: Intermediate Training

The commands in this chapter are a little more difficult, but your dog should be able to master them if they have mastered the ones in the previous chapter. Just remember to always be consistent, patient, and positive in your training!

Take It/Drop It

The take it and drop it commands are a great way to make the daily life with your pooch easier. You can have them take a toy, bone, or anything else you might need. But, more importantly, you can have them drop something. This is really helpful when you need to take something your dog isn't supposed to have, such as laundry, shoes, a broken toy, or anything else they might find. While this is helpful for all dogs, it is especially important for young and hyperactive dogs to learn, as they tend to be more destructive.

When training with this command, you want to practice trading low-value objects for high-value treats and objects. For instance, a low-value object might be a toy or a towel. You can then have them drop this low-value object for a high-value treat—whatever their favorite treat may be. This will teach your dog that while they may have to give away what they have, it will be worth it in the end.

Never chance your dog around or threaten them for an object. This will either make your dog believe you are playing a fun game of chase, encouraging them to keep going, or it will frighten them and damage your relationship with them. Instead, slowly walk up to your dog, peaceful and without emotion, and ask your dog to drop whatever they have. Once they do, reward them with the high-reward treats. While chasing your dog may seem like a way to get something important out of their mouth quickly, it really only delays the process. Instead, use this command. Of course, you have to first regularly practice and proof this command so that your dog learns to comply in any circumstance.

To teach 'take it/drop it,' follow these steps:

- Find an object that is low-value and hold it in front of your dog. When they open their mouth and begin to grab the object, say 'take it.'

- Allow your dog to play with the object for a minute before presenting them with a duplicate object of the same value.

- As your dog opens their mouth and the object they have falls out, say 'drop it.' Then reward them with the duplicate object. As they grab it with their mouth, say 'take it.' Practice and repeat this process regularly so that they learn the two command phrases.

- While practicing this, gradually up the value of the objects your dog is trading. This will help them learn to drop an object, even when they really want it. If they fail to drop the higher value item, say 'uh-oh' and walk away from them.

- Ignore them completely while you play with the object in your hand. Your dog will likely become curious about what you have, and then be more willing to trade for it. As soon as the drop the high-value toy, praise them and reward them with the item in your hand.

- Again, remember to always use the command words. Practice this command regularly.

Off

The 'off' command is great for when you need your dog to get off a piece of furniture, or even if they are sitting in your lap and you need them to get off. It is a much more effective and kind approach than pushing them.

To teach 'off,' follow these steps:

- When your dog is on a piece of furniture, whether completely or only with their front paws, lure them off with the treat. Allow them to see the treat that you have and hold it out of their reach so that they have to get off of the furniture in order to get it. The moment they get off, use the command word, praise them, and reward them.

- Practice using this command frequently, on a variety of furniture and situations, so that you can proof the command. If the dog doesn't want to get off a piece of furniture, say 'uh-oh,' and try again with a higher value treat.

- For a hand sign to go with this command, you can try pointing to the floor where you want your dog to go.

Quiet

There are many people who struggle with their dogs barking uncontrollably. For times likes this, 'quiet' is the perfect command. If you want to use a different word for this command, you might also consider using 'hush' or 'enough.'

To teach 'quiet,' follow these steps:

- First, trigger your dog's barking. There are different things that may cause a specific dog to bark. For some, it may be the doorbell; for others, it could be seeing other dogs on TV.

- When your dog begins to bark, quickly take a look at what your dog is barking at so that they know you are aware of whatever they are alerting you to. This could mean looking at the TV or looking out the window at your door.

- Now, go back to your dog and grab their attention with a high-value treat or toy. Once they fall silent, say the word 'quiet' before praising and rewarding them.

- Repeat this process multiple times, each time slightly lengthening the time that they have to be quiet in order to be rewarded. This helps them to learn that they have to stay quiet for more than just a moment.

- Whenever your dog is barking, practice using the command word, rewarding them with a high-value treat until they master complying with this command under any circumstance. Once they master the command, you can decrease the treat value.

Chapter 4: Advanced Training

The commands in this chapter are the most difficult, but they are incredibly helpful. You can start teaching your dog these commands no matter how young they are, even if they are still a puppy. But, because they are advanced, it will take a long time for a dog to master these commands under proofing. You have to remain patient, even if it takes a long time for your dog to comply with these commands as you would like.

Gentle

The gentle command is a great way to keep yourself and any other humans or pets safe around your dog. This can be helpful for any dog, but especially for larger and high-energy dogs who are more likely to accidentally injure others in their excitement. This command can help your dog calm down so that they stop mouthing, jumping, scratching, or any other behavior that can cause injury. For best results, begin practicing this command when your dog is as young as possible. Because this is an intermediate command, it may take a long time for your dog to master it, but by putting in the work early on, you will experience better results.

To teach 'gentle,' follow these steps:

- Begin practicing this command in a quiet environment free from distractions and after your dog has been fed a meal. This will help them calm down more easily, as they won't get as excited.

- Have your dog sit in front of you and hold a treat hidden in your fist. Allow your dog to examine your fist while saying the command word.

- If your dog begins to push at your hand with their paw, nibble it, or otherwise attempts to take the treat forcibly, say 'uh-oh,' while pulling your hand away.

- Present your hand again. If your dog gently noses or licks your hand, say 'gentle.' Praise and reward them with the treat. Repeat this process regularly.

- Gradually increase the value of the treats and the distractions to make the training more difficult.

- Once your dog has mastered being gentle with the food, then begin using this command in other circumstances. For instance, if your dog is being too rough when greeting you or playing, use the command again. Reward them if they do well, but if they don't say 'uh-oh,' and ignore them for a moment before trying again.

Wait

The wait command is great for when you want your dog to wait for something they desire. For instance, if you want them to wait before going out the door, before taking a treat, or before jumping up on furniture. With this command, your dog knows that they will get what they want, but they have to wait for it.

One great thing about the 'wait' command is that it is easy to practice during everyday life. Once they learn the basics, you don't have to set aside specific training sessions. You can find normal circumstances for them to wait, whether before going on a walk, before eating, or before taking a toy.

This command shouldn't be confused with 'leave it.' With 'wait,' your dog will eventually get what they want. On the other hand, with 'leave it,' your dog will not get what they want—they have to continue leaving it.

To teach 'wait,' follow these steps:

- Sit with your dog sitting a few feet in front of you.

- Show your dog that you have a treat and then place the treat on your knee while saying 'wait.'

- if your dog tries to take the treat, then pull it away and say 'uh-oh.' Repeat this process until your dog waits and doesn't try to take the treat.

- Make your dog wait for about three to four seconds and then in a happy and excited voice say 'okay' while pointing at the treat. Your dog should go for the treat now. After they get the treat, praise them.

- Repeat this many times, so that your dog learns the meaning behind 'wait.' Gradually increase the amount of time they have to wait.

- Once your dog waits for a length of time, begin proofing the behavior by mixing up distractions and the environment.

- After your dog has mastered waiting to take the treat, begin to teach them to wait in other instances. For this, it can be best to put your dog on a leash, to ensure they have to wait.

- After your dog is on a leash, walk them to the door, tell them to wait, and open the door. If they try to go out the door, then say 'uh-oh' while closing the door. Repeat this process until they will wait even once the door is open. After a few moments, say 'okay,' and go outside with your dog.

- Continue practicing the wait command in this way in as many circumstances as you can. You might also try having them wait before they eat, before coming out of their crate, before crossing the road, before getting on furniture, before taking a toy, or before greeting a person or animal. There are countless ways you can practice this command in your everyday life, and the more ways you find to practice it, the better and more useful it will be.

Leave It

This command is great for impulse control. You can use it in any circumstance to have your dog leave something they are not supposed to have. This can apply to shoes, food, or even a cat the dog might want to chase. Of course, you can't expect your dog to leave the object for all time. For instance, if you tell your dog to leave your shoes today, you can't expect them to continue leaving the shoes tomorrow. This command only works when used in specific circumstances.

It's impossible to overstate the importance of this command. That is because this command can keep both others and your dog safe. For example, you can have your dog leave toxic food such as chocolate or leave a small animal they might accidentally hurt.

This command shouldn't be confused with 'wait.' With 'wait,' your dog will eventually get what they want. On the other hand, with 'leave it,' your dog will not get what they want—they have to continue leaving it.

To teach 'leave it,' follow these steps:

•   While practicing this command, always have to sets of treats or toys. One is the item that the must leave, and the other is the one you will reward with. Never reward them with the item that you told them to leave, as this undermines the command. You want them to learn that they don't get the item that they leave at any point.

•   Have your dog sit a few feet in front of you. Hold your fist out, hiding a treat inside it. Hold your other hand behind your back with a treat for rewarding.

•   Allow your dog to sniff the treat that is extended in front of you. They will sniff, lick, and paw at your hand, trying to figure out how to get it. But, don't let them have it.

•   Wait for your dog to hesitate or move away momentarily. The moment your dog leaves the treat, even if only for a second, use the command word, praise them, and give them the reward treat that you had hidden behind your back.

- Repeat this process multiple times until your dog connects the word to the action.

- After your dog has built up a familiarity with the command word, practice saying 'leave it' the moment you present the treat in your hand to your dog. If they leave it, praise them and give them the hidden treat from behind your back. If they don't leave it, then say 'uh-oh,' pull your hand way momentarily, and try again.

Chapter 5: Puppy Training Basics

No matter the puppy, they need a solid foundation of learning so that they can grow into a healthy and happy adult dog with confidence. Without important teaching, your puppy would be unable to understand basic commands, which behaviors they should and shouldn't emulate, or how to interact with the outside world. Whether you are teaching your puppy through socialization, house training, or command prompts, by teaching your puppy now, they will be able to enjoy a more secure and happy life as your companion and friend. In this book, you will learn how to train your puppy, everything they need to achieve this goal.

Your puppy will be able to absorb your training, and they will be happy to learn as they will see the many benefits of positively working as a team rather than butting heads.

While some training methods can have puppies develop aggression and fear, the positive training method outlined in this book is just what you and your puppy need to live a secure and confident life. Your puppy will feel safe in knowing your love and care for them, and that they will be rewarded if they simply comply with your requests. There is no need for harsh words, choke collars, or physical threats that harm your relationship. You and your puppy can become a true team that works together for a better and happier life. By practicing the teachings in this book, your puppy will develop the foundational learning they need to achieve all this and more.

Just as humans can develop bad habits as they grow, so too can dogs. Even if you practice training your dog from the time they were a little puppy, they may still develop bad habits as they age. But, whether your dog has been trained as a puppy or you adult an adult dog with little to no training, you can help them overcome these bad habits and become a well-trained dog.

While some people claim that an old dog can't learn new tricks, this certainly isn't the case. Yes, the young years and months are an incredibly formative time in a puppy's life. But, that doesn't mean they can't be trained when they are older. In fact, many people adopt older dogs and then train them, rather than getting a puppy that is energetic and must be house trained.

Sadly, it can be difficult for people to know how to deal with some of the most common problem behaviors. These can arise due to a variety of reasons and manifest in many ways. Because of this, it can be confusing for the layman to know what to do. Thankfully, many dogs can be trained out of these behaviors—if their caregiver is willing to put in consistent effort. Before we get into the nitty-gritty of how to train your dog, let's look at some of the most common problem behaviors that can be lessened or completely overcome with proper training.

One of the biggest problems owners run into dogs that have behavior problems is aggression. This is because while aggression isn't necessarily more common than other behavior issues, it is the most dangerous problem. When a dog becomes aggressive, they become a danger to everyone around them—both human and animal. Because of this, many aggressive dogs end up seriously injuring those around them, surrendered to animal shelters; or worse, put down.

The way a dog displays their aggression can vary from case to case. Some dogs may specifically react to humans or other dogs, or they may only act aggressively when they are territorial or on a leash. It all depends on the cause of the dog's aggression, whether it is based on fear, anxiety, or insecurity.

Sadly, oftentimes, when training doesn't work to relieve aggression, it is because the root cause of the aggression was misdiagnosed. A person may believe that aggression is caused by a need to dominate and be the 'alpha' dog when that's not the case. But, when this type of belief is taught, people will try training their dogs with punitive methods, which only make the root cause and thus the aggression worse.

Punitive training ignores what a dog's true instinct is, mistaking their need for safety and family for dominance. The result is that rather than alleviating a dog's fear, anxiety, or insecurity, punitive training worsens these feelings of perceived danger. When the dog feels the perceived danger worsen, they will naturally become more aggressive in order to protect themselves from what they believe to be dangerous. Often times, it is not that the dog wants to hurt a person, but that they simply want to protect themselves.

In most cases, when a dog begins to show aggressive tenancies, it is because they don't know how to function in a domestic environment successfully. Because of this, they seek to protect themselves in the only way that they know how.

To protect themselves, a dog may lash out at other humans and animals if they approach the dog in question. But, they might also lash out in order to protect resources that they see as necessary for their health and well-being, such as food, furniture, space, or anything else that they see as 'theirs.' This is not because they are trying to dominate everyone and become an 'alpha,' but rather because they are scared to lose access to the resources they see as vital for their survival needs.

While the root cause of aggression is usually fear, anxiety, or insecurity, there are specific influences that can affect these feelings. These include:

1. Genetics
2. Age
3. Sex
4. Health
5. Hormone imbalance
6. Neural chemical imbalance
7. Whether or not they are spayed/neutered
8. Previous abuse or punitive 'training.'

When you want to help your aggressive dog, you should always be careful and stay safe. It is also wise to have your dog checked by a vet to see if there are any medical abnormalities that could be causing or worsening their aggression.

As you safely train an aggressive dog, the goal should be to treat the root cause of emotions that spur them on to act aggressively. This often means that you need to help them feel safe and secure so that they will see that they don't have to constantly be on guard, attempting to protect themselves. Help them see that there are no threats coming at them. Depending on the dog and the influences on their aggression, it may be a relatively short process, or it may take long, hard work. Every dog has their own pace of learning and growth. But, once you have trained your dog, the effects are likely to last, as positive reinforcement training has been found to be incredibly effective.

While positive training has great potential in helping dogs overcome their aggression, the same can't be said of punitive training. Often times, people turn to this type of training due to the flawed and outdated philosophies of preached by misguided trainers and TV stars.

But, what these programs don't reveal is that punitive training actually worsens a dog's aggression, as it only worsens the source of the aggression: their fear. In fact, these trainers and TV shows hide the fact that many people are injured by their dogs, specifically because of these misguided methods. For example, while attempting to 'dominate' their dog by forcibly holding them pinned to the floor, as certain punitive dog trainers have recommended on TV, many owners end up being bitten. In this case, it really isn't the dog's fault, as they were simply protecting themselves from the present danger their own owners posed. While the owner might not have any ill intent, they are physically displaying their control over the dog, which would scare anyone, especially a dog that is already struggling with fear.

When you decide to get a puppy, there are steps you must take before you bring your puppy home. First, it is always important that you don't make a choice to get a puppy lightly. Puppies are incredibly energetic and require a lot of hands-on-care and attention. Not only that, but even once your puppy grows into an adult dog and out of the puppy stage, they still require a commitment of up to twenty years, depending on the breed. Be sure that you or your family are willing to put in the time and effort your puppy will need for training, walks, mealtimes, attention, plus the monetary aspects of paying for any needs your puppy might have.

If you have decided that your home is the right place for a puppy and that you can commit to one, then congratulations! But what should you do now that you are looking for a puppy of your own? First, you need to decide whether you want to adopt or buy from a breeder, get a full-bred puppy or a mixed breed. There are benefits to both options, but it is always worth mentioning that there are many dogs and puppies in the shelter that need good homes. While many people look for purebred dogs, mixed breed dogs are just as great of an option. In fact, mixed-breed dogs can often have more balanced temperaments, and behaviors as the breed mixes can sometimes make up for weaknesses that a purebred dog would have.

When you go to find a puppy, whether, at a breeder or a shelter, you want to pay close attention to the temperament of the puppies available, if a puppy is overly shy or fearful, then it may have some temperament problems that will only deepen in the future. On the other hand, if the puppy comes right up to you or starts out a little shy before warming up, then that is a good sign of a puppy that can form healthy bonds and connections with others. This means that it is not necessarily bad if a puppy shows some signs of fear or shyness upon introduction. But, it all depends on whether the puppy is able to adapt to the circumstances and interact with you without fear or trepidation.

Take some time with the puppy. Any trustworthy shelter or breeder should allow you to spend time with the puppy so that you can decide if they are a good fit for your home. Watch closely to see how they interact with you and any other puppies around. See if they feel confident enough to play or cuddle with you. Will, the puppy, let your pet and hold them, or do they dodge your touch? Will they investigate anything new and novel, or do they shiver and hide in fear? How a puppy behaves now will impact how they age and develop in the future, so it is important that you watch them closely.

Along with watching the puppy yourself, try asking the shelter workers or breeder how the puppy behaves at other times. Do they play with the other puppies, hideaway, or bully the others? Are they friendly and warm, or shy and afraid? This can help give you some valuable insight into a puppy before you decide if their forever home belongs to you.

Keep in mind that no matter where you are getting a puppy from, whether a breeder, shelter, or a neighbor that accidentally wound up with a litter of puppies, you should never bring one home before they are at least seven weeks old. This is a vital time for a puppy to develop their natural instincts and socialization with other dogs. They will learn what is good and bad behavior by interacting with both their mother and siblings. If a person tries to convince you that a puppy can be adopted before seven weeks old, don't believe them and be wary of taking a puppy from them. This is an extremely bad practice that will harm the puppy for years to come, potentially for their entire life.

Once you bring your puppy home, it is time to start general training. I recommend and teach a positive training approach, as this helps dogs to have confidence and build a trusting bond with their owner. While harsh punitive training methods are used by a small selection of trainers, these are generally looked down upon as harmful. This is because these approaches teach a dog fear, aggression, and to fight back. Just as a child would harbor intense negative feelings if their parent pinned them to the ground and yelled in their face, a dog will experience the same emotions. Because of this, dogs that are taught with a punitive approach often become more aggressive, potentially biting their owner due to the fear instilled in them.

Many people believe that this punitive approach is natural and resembles a wolf pack, but that is not true. The original study in which researchers believed wolves to behave in a punitive manner toward other wolves was inaccurate, as it didn't study a genuine wolf pack. Instead, this study put a bunch of wild wolves from different packs and regions into an enclosure, which resulted in conflicts. It is easy to see how this study is inaccurate. Thankfully, through studying real wolf packs in the wild, researchers have been able to prove that wolves do not treat their pack members with aggression and fear-based tactics to be the "alpha dog." Instead, wolf packs show love and care toward each other, just like a family. When wolves do get into fights with each other, it is usually one pack fighting against another, rather than wolves within the same pack fighting.

Time and again, dog trainers have proven the positive training approach to be the superior method. This method creates a healthy bond between you and your dog, minimizes aggression, and encourages a dog to comply with demands so that they can experience a positive experience. Sometimes this positive experience they get in reward for behaving is a treat, but other times it is simply petting them and telling them "good dog," or throwing them a ball to play with. Your dog, or rather a puppy, will learn that be behaving and doing as you ask that you will be pleased and they will receive good things. Naturally, over time this will train your puppy to want to obey you.

Dogs are known as "man's best friend," as they share unconditional love with humans. With positive training, you can show your puppy that this unconditional love is mutual; that you love them just as much as they love you; that you will always take care of and protect them; that you won't get angry or abandon them. Seeing your love in action, your puppy will learn to trust you and love you even more, making them more than willing to please you through good behavior.

While every trainer's methods may vary slightly, there are four main elements central to positive training. These elements include the use of positive reinforcement, avoiding punitive training, understanding dominance, and seeking to understand your puppy's point of view. By understanding and embracing these four elements, you can train your puppy in a positive way that will benefit them and your relationship with them for years to come. Let's look more closely at each of these four elements in turn.

Used and accepted by a majority of expert dog trainers, positive reinforcement methods have been shown to be a humane, safe, effective, and long-lasting method of training. In fact, behavioral scientists have found this method to be superior to other options out there. With this method, you focus largely on positively reinforcing good behaviors that you want your dog to continue. Because of this, dogs learn that these good behaviors offer good rewards, making them more inclined to repeat them in the future. But, this doesn't mean you only ever praise your puppy. You can also take away rewards so that your puppy learns which behaviors you dislike. For instance, if your puppy won't stop barking for attention, you may turn your back on them and ignore them until they behave. By doing this, they will learn that they only get the reward (your attention) when they behave in the way you want. You may also try removing toys or food when a dog misbehaves. If they are really misbehaving, then you can even leave the room or put them in a separate room for two minutes or until they calm down. This short time away from you will teach the puppy really quickly.

Of course, removing rewards is much different than punitive training. With punitive and dominance training methods, people will punish a dog by yelling at them, physically pushing them around, or even shoving a dog's nose in their own mess. This should *never* happen and will only cause more problems. Positive training is different because it doesn't directly punish a dog with negative tactics; it simply takes away the rewards until your puppy continues to comply with your requests for positive behaviors. While the arguments for punitive training methods may seem compelling at first, when you look below the surface, you will see just how damaging they are. Not only do these methods have no science to back them up, but the opposite is actually true. Time and again, scientific studies have proven that punitive training methods have long-term negative consequences on a dog's behavior and temperament. This training method can make a dog aggressive, and exacerbate any preexisting aggression, making it an incredibly dangerous method. Remember, you should never fight fire with fire. While you may get frustrated with your puppy occasionally if they have a difficult spurt in their growth, never react with anger, confrontation, or a punitive method.

While science does prove that the punitive method can cause disastrous results while positive training yields success, it is common sense when you think about it. Dogs mentally process things similarly to the way toddlers do. As you might be aware, if a parent is unfair, unyielding, and overly punitive with their child, then the child is likely to rebel. A parent may do anything in the book to try to get their child to do what they say, but they simply won't win over the child's heart, and the child will continue to push back. It is the same with a dog. The more you fight your puppy, the more they will fight back in turn. But, if you encourage them to do the right thing with positive rewards, then they will be happy to comply. Afterward, they will only have a stronger bond with you, as they will appreciate your care.

Avoid any punitive training methods, such as physical intimidation, physically pushing or pinning your puppy, using shock or prong collars, yelling, or pushing your dog's nose into something. There are many different methods used in punitive approaches, but they are all harmful.

To understand your dog and their needs, you need to understand how dominance works with canines. Misunderstandings in dominance are common, especially due to the punitive training method that was popular in the early 2000s. This training method has mistakenly taught many people that they have to be the 'leader of the pack,' the 'alpha,' or the 'top dog.' These people have been taught that if they don't appropriately act like the 'alpha dog,' that their relationship with their dog will become unbalanced. But, as we previously mentioned, this is all based on an inaccurate early study on wolves. More recent and accurate findings have found that wolf packs do not rely on dominance to function. Yet, despite this knowledge being made public for some time, punitive dog trainers continue to ignore the truth and promote damaging training methods.

Your dog is not looking to rule your home or family. They are not trying to become the 'alpha' that will control you. Similarly, you don't have to act like an 'alpha' and dominate your dog, either. This doesn't create love, positive connections, or strong bonds. Rather, dominance will only tear these away and build fear and anxiety in their place.

Know that when your dog misbehaves, it is unlikely to be caused by a desire for dominance. Your dog is not acting out in order to gain control. Instead, when they misbehave, it is usually to fill a need of theirs. For instance, if your dog won't stop chewing on the furniture and remotes, it is likely because they are not getting enough physical or mental stimulation, or they don't have enough other toys and bones to chew on. If your puppy repeatedly nips at your hands when playing, it is because they have not learned the proper social skills and simply want to enjoy time with you. If your puppy has bathroom accidents, it is not on purpose, but because they either can not hold it or have not yet had enough training to know when and how to signal that they need to go outdoors. These are only a few instances, but there are countless ways that a person might believe their puppy is attempting to dominate when they are really just missing out on a need or training.

The last of the four elements to positive dog training is learning to understand your dog's point of view. In relationships, you can not truly form close bonds and connections unless you seek to understand the other person's point of view. This does not only apply to human relationships but all relationships, including those between human and canine. If you want to build connections with your dog and train them well, you must first attempt to understand how they view the world, their needs, how they communicate, and their experiences. By seeking to understand how your dog perceives the world around them, you can understand why they interact in the world in specific ways. This will allow you to then understand the best way to deal with misbehavior as well as making you more compassionate to their struggles. For instance, you can become more compassionate to your dog's barking if you understand that it is because they are stressed or lonely. Understanding the cause of the barking can then help you figure out how to overcome it. For instance, if your dog is stressed, you can narrow down what is causing them to be stressed and try to alleviate the problem. If your dog is lonely, you can make sure you give them plenty of attention during the day while also training them to not have anxiety when apart. Understanding one another is key to a sound relationship and successful interactions.

There are many different terms for positive-based training. For instance, people might also refer to it as reward-based, positive reinforcement, or force-free training. While these names may be different, they all abide by the four elements of positive training. In summary, let's look at some of the top benefits of positive puppy training.

9. Stronger Communication

While your dog may not be able to talk, the two of you can still communicate. After all, verbal communication only makes up a small percentage of all communication, with a majority of communication being made up of body language and tone of voice. These two forms of communication will allow you and your puppy to communicate without words. While punitive training methods punish dogs and rely fully on negative and abusive communication, with positive training, you can truly practice open and positive communication with your puppy. All you have to do is be willing to "listen" to your dog's communication through their actions and body language, and in turn, communicate in a way that they can understand.

10. Create Strong Bonds

When you bring home your puppy, you want to create a strong family bond with it. Whether you are the sole owner of the puppy, or it is going to be a family dog, strong bonds are important for healthy and happy relationships. If a person practices punitive style training, then it will result in a damaged relationship. Your dog won't be able to trust you, and they will come to expect violence and aggression. On the other hand, if you practice positive training, your puppy will learn that you are the source of everything good. That whenever they get attention, treats, toys, or playtime, it all is because you care for them. This will naturally create strong bonds where they love and appreciate you, and because of this, they will be more inclined to do as you ask.

11. Treat and Prevent Behavior Problems

Punitive training methods have been proven by researchers and in studies to cause behavior problems originating from aggression, anxiety, and fear. Even more so, if your dog already has these behavior problems, then punitive methods will only make them worse. But, while punitive training methods may cause behavior problems, studies have also found that positive-based training is frequently successful in preventing and overcoming such problems.

12. Family Activities

Unlike punitive-based training, which can be dangerous, positive training can get the whole family involved! Even young children can be shown how to use simple positive training methods, allowing them to help train your new puppy. This is great for many reasons. It will allow your puppy and child to develop stronger dogs, help your puppy learn how to listen to your child's commands, and it can teach your child responsibility. Just make sure that an adult fully explains to the child what they should and shouldn't do to ensure they don't unknowingly make harmful mistakes. Depending on the age and maturity of your child, these training sessions might have to be adult-supervised to make sure they aren't making mistakes without you being aware.

13. Get Some Exercise

Dogs—and especially puppies—have a lot of energy. In fact, many people don't realize just how much energy these furry friends have. This can cause confusion when a dog starts developing behavior problems seemingly out of nowhere, as the owner might not realize the puppy is simply not getting enough physical and mental stimulation. Positive training is able to help you overcome this difficulty by giving your puppy an outlet for both mental and physical stimulation. Even just five minutes of training can give your puppy some much needed mental stimulation and decrease problem behaviors.

14. **Have Fun While You Train**

> If you have ever used punitive training methods, you are likely aware of all the aggression and anxiety it can breed in both humans and canines. Fun is the furthest thing from punitive training. But, this is not the case with positive training. You and your dog can have fun together, making a game out of it! Your dog will come to learn training sessions, as it will mean they get plenty of rewards and one-on-one attention for doing as you ask. In turn, you will have fun seeing your dog excited, praising them for doing well. For instance, if you are teaching your dog the "sit" command, they will become excited every time you give the command because they know if they comply, you will reward them in their favorite way. This makes training fun for everyone involved.

After Bringing Your Puppy Home

Now that we have explored the method of positive-based training and its benefits, let's look at some ways you can help get your puppy settled in at home. By getting your puppy started off on the right foot, you can experience success in training earlier, making the energetic puppy stages easier to manage.

When you first bring your puppy home, make sure that everything is in order. You want to puppy-proof any area that your puppy will be so that they don't have anything dangerous they may chew on or eat. You should also have a designated area for puppy potty pads. While you may have relatives or friends who want to come over and visit the newest addition to your family, try to discourage anyone from coming over at least on the first day. It is best to save this time to allow your puppy to acclimate and get to know you without too much stress.

While taking your puppy outside to go potty, take them out on a leash and walk them to the specific spot you want them to do their business in. This will help later on, for when you begin potty training. It will also help them learn to go potty whenever you specifically walk them to that area so that you don't have to walk around the entire yard late at night, waiting for them to do their business.

Create a safe space for your puppy where their bed is located. Remember, dogs are den animals. Therefore they need their own den in order to feel safe and secure in an area. Without this, they will feel more anxious and on edge, possibly leading to problem behaviors. It is best to make this area a quiet space where they can be completely alone whenever they need to nap.

As they are a puppy, they will require plenty of these nap times, just like a baby. In this quit, den adds a bed, some toys for chewing, a potty pad, and a crate. Let your puppy stay in this den whenever they are sleeping, whether for a nap or at bedtime. This will let your puppy learn that whenever they are in that space, it is time to settle down and rest, creating good and helpful habits for the future.

Introducing the New Dog

If you have other pets at home, keep them and your new puppy separate for a few days. You want to allow your puppy to feel safe and secure in their new environment before they begin meeting other pets. This is vital, as it will improve their interaction and increase the chance of a successful meeting. When you do introduce your puppy to your other pets, you want to do it in as neutral of an area as possible; this means don't introduce them at the puppies or one of your other pet's bed area. Instead, it is generally best to introduce them in a common room or in the backyard.

When you do introduce them, keep your pets on a leash, when possible. This may not be possible if you are introducing your puppy to a cat, but at the very least, keep your puppy on a leash. The leashes are important, in case one of your pets becomes overwhelmed by the introduction. The least will allow you to easily help your pets disengage if they are stressed or not getting along, without causing injury to anyone involved. Sometimes pets will get along right away, but sometimes the introduction process is a slow process ongoing for weeks at a time. It really depends on your specific pets, so don't expect them to get along immediately.

When you do introduce your pets, make sure that they are always supervised until you can completely trust them to get along at all times. Even if things seem great at first, you want to at least supervise their time together for the first week or two, until you can fully trust that neither of them will become overwhelmed or accidentally hurt the other.

Have Realistic Expectations

Always keep in mind that you shouldn't treat your puppy as if they were an adult dog. You may become overwhelmed if you see your puppy peed in the house, smeared poop all over their crate, chewed up your couch, or nipped at your hands. But, these are normal mistakes you run into when raising a puppy.

Just as you can't expect an infant or a toddler to act like an adult, you can't expect a puppy, too, either. They will make mistakes, but they will learn in time. Similarly, don't expect them to outgrow this puppy stage too quickly. Even after your puppy stops growing, it can take a puppy two years to reach adult dog maturity. Offer them compassion and patience for their mistakes, and then kindly continue their training addressing your concerns.

While you can't expect your puppy to act like an adult right away, you can begin training them much earlier than you might expect. Many people wait to train their puppies until they are a few months old, but this wastes valuable time. By wasting this time, your puppy will start to develop poor habits, rather than the good habits you want to instill. The good news is that you can start training your puppy as soon as they come home, as early as seven weeks old! Of course, you can't expect too much of a puppy at this age, but they can learn basic commands and behaviors. Keep these training sessions, especially short, no more than five minutes at a time. But, while the training sessions might be short, you can practice them regularly throughout the day. Try to practice these sessions specifically when your puppy has enough energy, avoiding doing so when they are tired or frustrated. If they become frustrated and start to struggle with complying with your commands, don't continue the training session. You want to keep these sessions positive and end them on a good note so that your puppy develops a good association with training.

Practice Makes Perfect

When practicing your training session, as previously mentioned, they should only be five minutes long for especially young puppies. But, as your puppy matures, you can slowly lengthen them, until training sessions are up to twenty minutes long. Don't go longer than this, as it takes a lot of concentration for your dog and twenty minutes it a long time, even for an adult and fully mature dog.

One of the first things you should do as practicing your training sessions is determining what your puppy's favorite reward methods are. The main rewards are attention, play, toys, and treats. As you practice training and simply get to know your puppy better, you should be able to rank each of these reward methods from favorite to least favorite. For instance, you might find that they are especially motivated by food and less motivated by toys, or vice versa. By coming to understand your puppy's favorite rewards, then you can better know what methods to use when training them. Once you discover these methods, then try to find sub-categories of these rewards. For instance, you can test a variety of treats to see which your dog is most motivated by. They might absolutely love liver treats while carrots are enjoyed but not as special.

While some treats may be liked by your puppy more than others, this does not mean that the lesser value treats serve no value. Use the highest value treats as a "jackpot" treats for when your puppy is doing especially well, learning something especially difficult, or need extra motivation. You can then use carrots, and lesser value treats for easier commands.

By doing this, you ensure the high-value treats are continued to be viewed as special, as they are not always expected.

Chapter 6: House Training and Problem Behaviors

In the previous chapter, we discussed the basics of positive training for your puppy. One of the many great things about positive puppy training is that when used regularly and correctly, it can prevent and manage many everyday problematic puppy behaviors. For instance, you can teach your puppy impulse control, how to play without doing it roughly, alternatives to nipping and biting, when it's inappropriate to bark, and much more.

Now that we have established the importance of positive-based training, its benefits, and how to begin practicing this training method, we will discuss how you can begin training your puppy in basic behaviors. This includes house training your puppy and helping them overcome problem behaviors, such as whining and biting.

Biting

When puppies are young, they tend to have a habit of chewing, biting, and nipping. The reason they do this is to help them explore and understand the world better and to play. This behavior is especially problematic when they are teething, and they feel a constant need to chew to relieve the pressure. But, if you are not careful, this can set up bad habits for the future. While it may be cute now, it quickly becomes problematic and painful. The last thing you want is an adult dog with a biting habit, so it is best to nip it in the bud early on through training. Thankfully, you can teach your puppy boundaries early on through training, which will instill the correct behaviors in them into adulthood.

I like to start by teaching a puppy the command 'good kisses.' With this command, you can help a puppy learn that while biting isn't appreciated, they can '*kiss*,' or lick your hand instead. This is especially helpful with mouthy puppies, as it still gives them an outlet to interact with your hand. To teach this command, simply praise your puppy and say the cue phrase, 'good kisses,' whenever they give you a kiss. Once they have associated the phrase with the action, start giving them the command first. During a training session, say 'good kisses,' and wait for your puppy to kiss you. Once they do, exuberantly praise them and give them a reward. Practice this regularly until your puppy gives you kisses without hesitation.

Now, when your puppy starts mouthing you, yelp in a high-pitched voice and pulls your hand away. This yelp is effective, as it is the same signal a mother dog and your puppy's litter mates would use to communicate that a bite hurt. If you do this whenever your puppy mouths you, they will learn that it is painful and be less likely to do it in the future. After your puppy stops mouthing you, you can follow it by the command 'good kisses,' and praise them for giving you a kiss instead. Over time, they should learn that giving kisses is preferable to mouthing. Whenever they do mouth, you can simply yelp or say 'no,' and remind them to give you a kiss instead.

It is also important for a puppy to learn that they will never get what they want if they are mouthing. Often times, a puppy will nip and bite at a person or their clothing when they want to play. Even if you start getting frustrated with your puppy, they will likely only continue. This is because even though you are giving them negative attention by being frustrated, you are still giving them some form of attention, which is what they want. Therefore, instead of getting frustrated as they won't stop nipping, you should do the opposite of what they want. Since they are trying to get you to play, instead you should turn your back and walk away from them without even looking at them. You only need to leave them for thirty to sixty seconds to get the message, though sometimes you will need to repeat this process a few times until your puppy realizes that you won't give in.

Never agree to play with your puppy if they begin mouthing. The moment they start nipping or biting, get up and walk away, ending the playing session. You can wait a minute and then resume playing, but never continue while they are mouthing. Of course, you should supply your puppy with plenty of alternatives to chew on. If you don't want your puppy to be chewing on you or your furniture, then provide them with plenty of bones and chew toys. These are incredibly important for a puppy's developmental process, especially during the teething months.

When your puppy starts mouthing on you, don't even tell them 'no.' While this attention may be short and negative, it is still giving them some amount of attention. Instead, always just turn around and walk away. Although this is mainly only during the learning stage, once your puppy is older and has well-established that they don't mouth, they might occasionally make a mistake. When this happens, you can tell them 'no,' and remind them to give 'good kisses,' instead. But, if your puppy won't listen to the 'no,' or they haven't fully established the no-biting rule, then you should simply ignore them without the use of any command words.

Whining and Crying

When you bring your new puppy home, one behavior you can expect is whining and crying. Anyone who grew up watching Lady and the Tramp can remember the classic scene where Lady wound up crying through the night. While Lady's owners started out intent on letting her cry it out and not giving in, it didn't last long. Before long, they let Lady out, and it created a habit for the rest of her life. This scene may be from a movie, but it is a classic scenario that happens in a home when people bring a new puppy into the family. First off, never punish your puppy for whining. This also means you should not use pain or intimidation. As we discussed in the previous chapter, this punitive style training only causes long-term problems for both humans and canines. Remember, your puppy's whining does serve a purpose. They use it to communicate a need or desire. Your job as their caretaker is to address any needs they might have, such as taking them out to do their business or providing fresh food and water. Then, if they are crying because of a desire rather than a need, you can teach them the correct behavior. For instance, you can teach your puppy that instead of crying at bedtime, they are meant to lay down and rest. That even if they do cry, you won't let them out of bed, unless they truly need something.

Let's look at some ways you can address your puppy's whining and cry:

- Whenever your puppy is whining, listen closely to distinguish the tone of the whining and any other behaviors that may be accompanying it. This is important, as it can inform you as to why your puppy is whining. Of course, when your puppy first comes home, you won't be able to tell the difference in tone and what a puppy needs, but as you get to know your puppy better, you will be able to distinguish their cries. This will help you know when their whining is because they're lonely, bored, need something, stressed, or injured.

- It can be easy to rush to your puppy to care for them whenever you hear them whining, but it is important to look at the situation objectively. Listen closely to their whine and determine why they might be whining before you act.

- If you suspect your puppy may be crying due to injury or stress, approach and handle it carefully to avoid causing further distress or harm. Check on your puppy to make sure it is okay, and get it any care it might need.

- Your puppy might be whining because they are stressed or fearful of something. If this is the cause, try to find out what is affecting your dog. There are countless causes for fears, anxieties, and phobias, and only by knowing your dog will you be able to figure out what is causing your dog's reaction. For instance, it may be that they are scared of a specific object in the room or a noise they can hear from outside. If something specific is scaring your dog, then try taking it away, and later on, you can work on desensitizing training.

- While you don't want to reward your dog for whining, if your dog has a specific need, then it is your job to provide it. For instance, if they need food, water, a potty break, or an environment that makes them feel safe, then you can give them what they need.

- Yes, you need to meet your dog's needs, but you shouldn't give in to their 'wants' so easily. If they simply desire something, such as attention, play, or to stay awake, then giving in to their desire will create bad habits. Your puppy will learn that they can annoy and guilt you into giving them whatever they want, even if it isn't for the best.

- Try to avoid encouraging your dog to whine. If you know, they want something that doesn't reward the whining by giving into what they want. Instead, you can redirect their behavior first. For instance, if you know your puppy wants to play, you can have them sit still and quiet for a moment. You can then reward them for being good by playing with them, as they wanted.
- A puppy is more likely to whine if they have the pent up physical and mental energy. Just like a child, a puppy needs stimulation for both mind and body. Enrich their environment to meet these needs by giving them toys, taking them on walks, playing, and having regular training sessions.

- If your dog is whining, but there is no real need, then it is best to ignore their cries. You can wait for your dog to be quiet for a moment, and then use the command "quiet" and praise and reward them. After they associate the command with the action of being quiet, you can then use the command in the future to stop noisy behavior.

House Training

One of the first things you will likely be doing once your puppy is settled into their new home and family is house training. Depending on the methods used, a person's schedule, and your individual puppy, it can either be a quick and easy or a long and time-consuming process. Thankfully, if you use common sense, positive reinforcement, and most important—consistency, then you can have a fully house-trained puppy in the near future. The area you most need to be consistent in when house training is in your puppy's potty schedule. It is vital that you have this schedule in which you consistently take your puppy outside. This schedule will ensure your puppy's bladder doesn't get too full, leading to accidents. But that is not all. The puppy will also learn the schedule, which will encourage them to 'hold it' until their next time outside. Before long, going potty outside will become a habit, and they will be unlikely to make as many accidents.

Keep in mind that it is helpful to use a crate for house training. A puppy won't want to soil their bedding, which will encourage them to hold their bladder when at night, nap times, and whenever you leave them at home. Of course, there is a limit to how long a puppy can hold it. In general, a puppy can be expected to hold their bladder about one hour for each month of age. This means that if your puppy is three months old, then they should be able to hold their bladder for three hours. Of course, this will vary slightly based on your individual dog. An adult dog can be expected to hold their bladder up to eight to ten hours.

Please always remember that mistakes happen. Even if you take your puppy out regularly, they may make a mistake. This could be a simple mistake of your puppy peeing on the floor after nap time. But, more stressful mistakes have been known to happen—such as puppies pooing in their crates overnight, then left stressed and overwhelmed because they are distraught by the mess. Just as the puppy is distraught to be in their own filth, their owner is also left stressed out, having to clean up the mess.

When mistakes do happen, never punish your puppy. They are not at fault, no matter the circumstance. This is simply a part of house training and something you signed up for when you decided to bring a puppy into your family. Don't scold your puppy, speak to them in harsh words, give them the cold shoulder, or push their nose in their mess. Punishing your puppy for their biological needs is never a good idea, no matter how you do it. If you are able to catch your puppy in the act of soiling in the house, then you can try to stop the behavior without punishment. To do this, make a startling yelp sound, without scaring your puppy. Then pick up your puppy and say 'outside' as you carry them out. Place them in their designated potty area and give them the word to continue, whether that is 'potty,' 'do your business,' or anything else. Allow your puppy to finish, and then praise them and give them treats for doing well. This is important, as you don't want your puppy to think they will get into trouble for doing what they must. Otherwise, they will try to hide it from you, which will only cause trouble in the future.

If you find a soiled area in your house, be sure to clean it thoroughly immediately. Puppies will naturally want to go back to the same spot to do their business again, so you want to be sure you completely get rid of the smell so that it doesn't lead to further mistakes, or worse, a habit. When house training your puppy, try to keep close supervision over them so that they don't soil indoors. If you notice your puppy begins to sniff around, raise their leg, squat, white, or go toward the outside door, then immediately take them outside to do their business.

If you are unable to supervise your puppy, then try to keep them in a confined area. This confined area can either be a crate for bedtime or a fenced-off area with puppy pads in it. The fenced-off area and puppy pads are a great option for extended periods when you might not be home, as it will allow your puppy to have a spot to eat, drink, sleep, play, and do their business during the day. Although, it is best to avoid this at night, as they can better learn to hold their bladder overnight when in a crate fit for their size needs.

Now, let's look at the vital points you should take your puppy out for a potty break during house training.

Chapter 7: Socialization Training

In this chapter, we will be getting your puppy started on the right foot with important beginner training every puppy should know. This includes basic teachings for a well-behaved puppy, such as socialization and automatic defense training.

Socialization Benefits

One vital aspect of growth for any living creature is touch. Whether you are talking about a baby or a puppy, they need a touch from others to help them learn how to interact in the world around them. This first touch usually comes from the mother, who will care for them, feed them, and teach them what they should and shouldn't do to stay safe and healthy. The mother dog will lick and nuzzle her puppies to comfort them, bond with them, and promote circulation. The litter of puppies will sleep, eat, and play together, learning how to interact with others safely.

It is these interactions that teach a puppy what type of play is fun and what is harmful, as the fellow puppies and the mother dog will yelp if one of the puppies plays too roughly. This is just one of many lessons that puppies are taught in their first seven to eight weeks of life before they find their forever homes. If a puppy doesn't get this vital interaction, then it can make the learning process more difficult and time-consuming as they age—though not impossible.

But, this type of socialization for your puppy doesn't stop when they turn eight-weeks-old. If you want your puppy to learn how to interact safely with the people, animals, and the world around them, then you must continue to socialize them and promote healthy boundaries as they age.

Studies have even found that when a puppy is taken away from their mother and litter before seven or eight weeks old that they are more likely to develop life-long negative traits. This includes nervousness, hyperactivity, fear, and even aggression. Suffice it to say; you never want to trust a breeder who is willing to give you a puppy any earlier than seven weeks of age.

Early Socialization

You want to begin socializing your puppy as early as possible once they come home so that you can set up good behaviors and habits from the beginning. If you put socializing off, it can cause long-term anxiety and fear in your puppy, which can show themselves in many ways. Your dog may become so anxious about going to the vet that they shake uncontrollably, get high blood pressure, and are unable to keep food down. Or, they might be so scared of meeting other people or dogs that they react aggressively, as they are just trying to protect themselves from someone they see as a possible danger.

After your puppy has a few days or a week to settle into their new environment in your home, you want to begin introducing them to new sights, smells, sounds, people, animals, and experiences. There is a whole world out there, and if you don't want them to be fearful of it, then you need them to learn to take new encounters without fear but rather as a natural way of life. With practice, they will find that these new experiences can be positive experiences, rather than fearful or negative experiences. You will want to think of as many new experiences for them to interact with as possible, try making a list!

You especially want to focus on experiences they might encounter with your lifestyle. For instance, if you live on a farm, then you might want to allow them to experience being around larger animals. If you live in the city, then you want to experience walking on the sidewalk while there are loud vehicles going by. There are many other types of experiences, too. You want them to meet people of different races, wearing different clothing items and styles, and with different scents. You want them to meet small and large dogs, and even cats if possible. You want your puppy to adjust to encountering new objects, whether it is an umbrella or a large box fan. You can even make a game of this, hiding treats around new items or creating a scavenger hunt.

Keep in mind that you always want to make these experiences positive, as a negative experience can increase fear and anxiety, potentially for your puppy's entire life. This is especially important when puppies are young, as between eight to ten weeks, when puppies tend to go to their new homes, they are in a vulnerable state when they are more prone to becoming fearful of new experiences. Often times, this is known as a puppy's 'fear period.' While you should always be careful to keep socialization positive, this is especially true during specific developmental stages, such as the fear period. Similarly, if your puppy undergoes a stressful event during the first four to six months of their life, this can greatly affect their confidence and temperament.

Positivity is Key

One part of keeping socialization positive is to be careful not to overwhelm your puppy with too many experiences. You want to create a balance of allowing your puppy to experience enough during this stage so that they are properly socialized, but without overwhelming them. If a puppy becomes overwhelmed with the experience, it can have the opposite of the intended consequence, causing the puppy to experience more fear in the future. Take things slowly, reward your puppy regularly, and if you notice your puppy is getting stressed from a situation, gently pull them out of it. Don't reward the stress or baby them, but gently care for them while providing for their emotional and physical needs. You can always try a specific socialization exercise again later if the first attempt didn't work out.

Now, to make your socialization training successful, let's have a look at some tried-and-true tips and tricks.

Socialization Tips and Tricks

- You want your puppy to learn how to cope with new experiences, no matter who they are with. To do this, you can get the entire family involved in the socialization process. Try allowing your puppy to experience new things when they are with different family members. You can even make a list of what things your puppy has experienced, and which things you still want them to experience during this formative time. For instance, you may allow them to experience riding in the car, being near a bicycle, or hearing certain loud noises. By experiencing these with the entire family, rather than with just one person, your puppy can learn to always expect and calmly handle new experiences no matter which person they are with at the time.

- Don't rush the socialization process. While it is vital that you don't put it off and waste the important growth stage for your puppy to learn and grow, you don't want to overwhelm them. This not only means that you should pull your puppy out of situations that are overly stressful or getting out of control, but also that you shouldn't introduce too many new things all at once. While you may want to keep going once you get the ball rolling, you should always take baby (or puppy) steps. Try to limit new exposures for your puppy to only a few small experiences or one large experience a day. An example of small experiences is baseball caps, sunglasses, or bicycles. On the other hand, a large experience would be going to the pet store, vet, or meeting new people.

- When you begin socialization, you want to do this in an environment that your puppy is comfortable in. This means you should start with small experiences at home. Once your puppy is confident with these small experiences, you can begin to socialize them outside of the home, where there are more unpredictable events. This can include taking your puppy on walks, to the pet store, to the vet, to a friend's house, or to a play date with a friend's dog. Keep in mind that your puppy shouldn't go to the pet store or interact with other animals until after that have gotten their vaccinations.
- While you can certainly train your puppy on your own, you still might want to consider taking your puppy to behavior classes once they have their vaccinations. These classes are not only great because they help owners train their puppies, but because they give your puppy valuable socialization experiences. They can learn to interact with other people

and dogs in a safe environment. You can find local behavior training schools in your area or try out the training classes by PetSmart.

- Always remember that when socializing your puppy, your first priority is to make the experience positive. To do this, you want your puppy to feel safe and reward them for confident and curious behavior. It is also important to avoid babying your puppy if they get startled while still pulling them out of an overly stressful experience. This takes careful balance. But, if you learn to communicate and understand your puppy, then you will be able to recognize when they have general light stress from a new situation or when the situation is overwhelmingly stressful.

Chapter 8: Crate Training

Crate training is a great way to keep your puppy from getting into trouble at night and nap time, as well as an aid in the house training process. If you practice crate training your puppy while also house training them, you can better encourage them to hold their bladder. This works, because puppies won't want to soil the same space they use for their bed. In fact, if a puppy is unable to hold it and ends up being forced to soil their bed, then they can become quite distressed with the mess.

As their caretaker, it will be your job to take them out frequently, to try to avoid this. But, mistakes do happen, and at some point, your puppy may not be able to hold it as long as they would usually be able to, for whatever reason. If this happens, don't get upset with your puppy, simply take them outside to see if they have any business left to do, clean them up, and then clean up their bed and crate.

If you have to leave the house or briefly leave your puppy unattended, then putting them in the crate is a great way to prevent them from getting into any trouble. This is especially great for young puppies, which require frequent naps, as they are more likely to settle down and rest. While putting your puppy in a 'cage' may not sound like the best option, there really are many benefits!

Crating Basics

First, the crate is meant to act as your puppy's den. Naturally, dogs are den animals, and having a den makes them feel safe and secure, especially if there is something stressful going on. Your puppy may be unsure about a crate at first because it is something new, but with a little training, they can come to love their crate. There are many dogs who will happily run to their crate at nap time, bedtime, or whenever they are feeling stressed, all because they know it is a comfortable and safe spot to rest. By establishing the crate as a safe haven now, you can have it ready in case a stressful event occurs in the future.

When purchasing a crate for your puppy, you don't want to get one that is too big. While it may sound nice to get one that they will grow into, this will only hinder the house training process. This is because house training with a crate relies on the fact that your puppy won't want to soil their own bed. But, if the crate is big enough for them to grow into, then they can soil one end of the crate while still sleeping on the other end. The general rule of thumb when purchasing a crate is to get one big enough for your dog to stand up fully in, but not so much that they have room to walk around.

Getting Started

While there are many puppies who love their crate, upon the first inspection, a puppy will likely be unsure or even fearful of a crate. This makes sense; puppies need a lot of socialization in order to feel secure and confident. A crate is larger than the puppy, looks odd, and you want them to get into it. It's no wonder it may appear untrustworthy upon first glance. But, if you give your puppy the chance to become acquainted with their crate, they will likely develop a fond affection for their new den and bed.

To introduce your puppy first place their bed and some toys inside it, so that it looks comfortable and inviting. This will also help add their scent to the crate, making it smell less foreign. Sit on the floor with your puppy and leave the crate door open. Don't push them to get into it, but rather allow them to investigate it on their own. After your puppy has had a couple of minutes to adjust to sitting next to the crate, try luring them into it by tossing treats inside. Depending on your puppy, they may follow after the treats immediately, or they may take quite a while. Allow them to take their time, don't force them into the crate as that will only increase their fear and trepidation. Once they go inside, allow them to settle down or investigate without closing the door, so that they don't feel locked in. Allow them to stay or leave, whichever makes them feel safe.

After your puppy is comfortable going in and out of the crate with the use of rewards practice closing the door behind them. At first, you only want to close the door for a few seconds, so that they know they aren't trapped. But, as your puppy becomes more relaxed, you should gradually increase this time. Eventually, you want to get to them being in the crate with the door closed, and you present for ten to fifteen minutes.

Introducing Isolation

Once your puppy can comfortably stay in the crate with you in the room, it is time for you to train them to stay comfortable without you present. This time, put them in the crate like usual, but instead of staying in the room left. You only want to leave for one minute before coming back and letting your puppy out with plenty of praise and rewards. Continue practicing, gradually leaving the room for longer periods until you can leave for at least thirty minutes. While this may seem like a long time, it is usually easy, as by this point, your puppy will be comfortable in their crate, and they will likely fall asleep to take a nap. Remember never to rush any training, including crate training. Some puppies simply need more time to adjust, and that is okay. This process may take only a few hours for some puppies, but days for others.

When you first begin crate training, you need to decide on a command word, such as 'crate,' 'bed,' 'den,' or 'place.' Then, every time your puppy walks into their crate, use the command word, praise them, and give them a reward. There are two benefits to this. First, it will create a positive association with the crate so that your puppy learns to love their crate and find it to be a comfortable and safe space. Second, this will teach your puppy the command word so that you can use it in the future whenever you need them to go into the crate. This is not only helpful at bedtime, but also whenever you have company coming over, or a sudden unexpected event occurs (such as broken glass), and you need your puppy to be safe and out of the way. Remember, as always, you must use the command while they are completing the action on multiple occasions. You can't simply give them the command and expect them to know what to do before conditioning.

Keep in mind that you should never force your puppy into their crate, as this will only create a negative association. If you are having a hard time getting them into the crate, then try thinking of it from their point of view. What might be keeping them out of the crate, and are they motivated enough? If the problem is simply motivation, then you might try tossing some toys or treats into the crate. If you think your puppy might be refusing in order to get attention, then try leaving the room for a minute, coming back, and trying again. You might have to do this a few times, but after a few attempts, you will likely find your puppy more willing. Just be sure that once they do go into the crate, you stop ignoring them and instead offer them some much-deserved praise and rewards. Similarly, you should never use the crate as a punishment for mistakes or 'bad' behavior. Again, the crate is meant to be a positive and safe space, not a grounding zone.

While it may be tempting to leave your puppy in the crate in the mornings so that you can get coffee and breakfast before taking them outside, never do this. If you leave your puppy in the crate longer than they can handle, then they are more likely to soil it. If they do this, they will be more likely to soil it in the future, making house training more difficult. Similarly, never leave your puppy in the crate for overly long periods. They can not handle being in it all day, as it will cause hyperactivity, stress, anxiety, and a host of bad behaviors as a result.

Crate Tips

- Keep a comfortable bed and safe toys in the crate.
- Avoid toys and bones that require supervision.
- Always use the same command word for the crate.
- Be patient when crate training. Don't rush the process.
- If your puppy whines or barks in the crate waiting for them to be quiet before you let them out.
- Create a positive association by feeding your puppy meals in their crate.

- Remove any food or water from the crate at bedtime, so that they don't soil it overnight. But, always provide them water during the day and ensure they get enough to drink before bedtime.

Conclusion

Whether you are still deciding whether you should bring a puppy into your family, have just come home with a wiggling little jellybean of your own, or are a few months into your puppy journey—the knowledge in this book can help you. You now have the knowledge you need to experience the joys that come with parenthood to your own little puppy, as you have the knowledge to succeed. With time, as you see, the practices taught in this book implemented into your puppy's life; both you and your puppy will find a new sense of confidence.

You no longer have to worry about which method of training is the best, how to house train, socialize, deal with problem behaviors, or crate train. You have the knowledge you need, and all you have to do it take the next step to implement it. If you ever run into problems, refer back to the pages of this book for guidance, as you will be surprised how often problems occur from simple mistakes. This book is here for you, as a guide and help through the ups and downs as your puppy ages.

If you follow the advice found in the book, you will find that both you and your puppy can have a happier and healthier life together. All you have to do is be patient, show love, and follow the information step-by-step.

www.ingramcontent.com/pod-product-compliance
Lightning Source LLC
Chambersburg PA
CBHW071749080526
44588CB00013B/2196